The **mail carriers** are special helpers
Who bring us all our mail.
They deliver almost every day;
They do it without fail.

Color the picture.

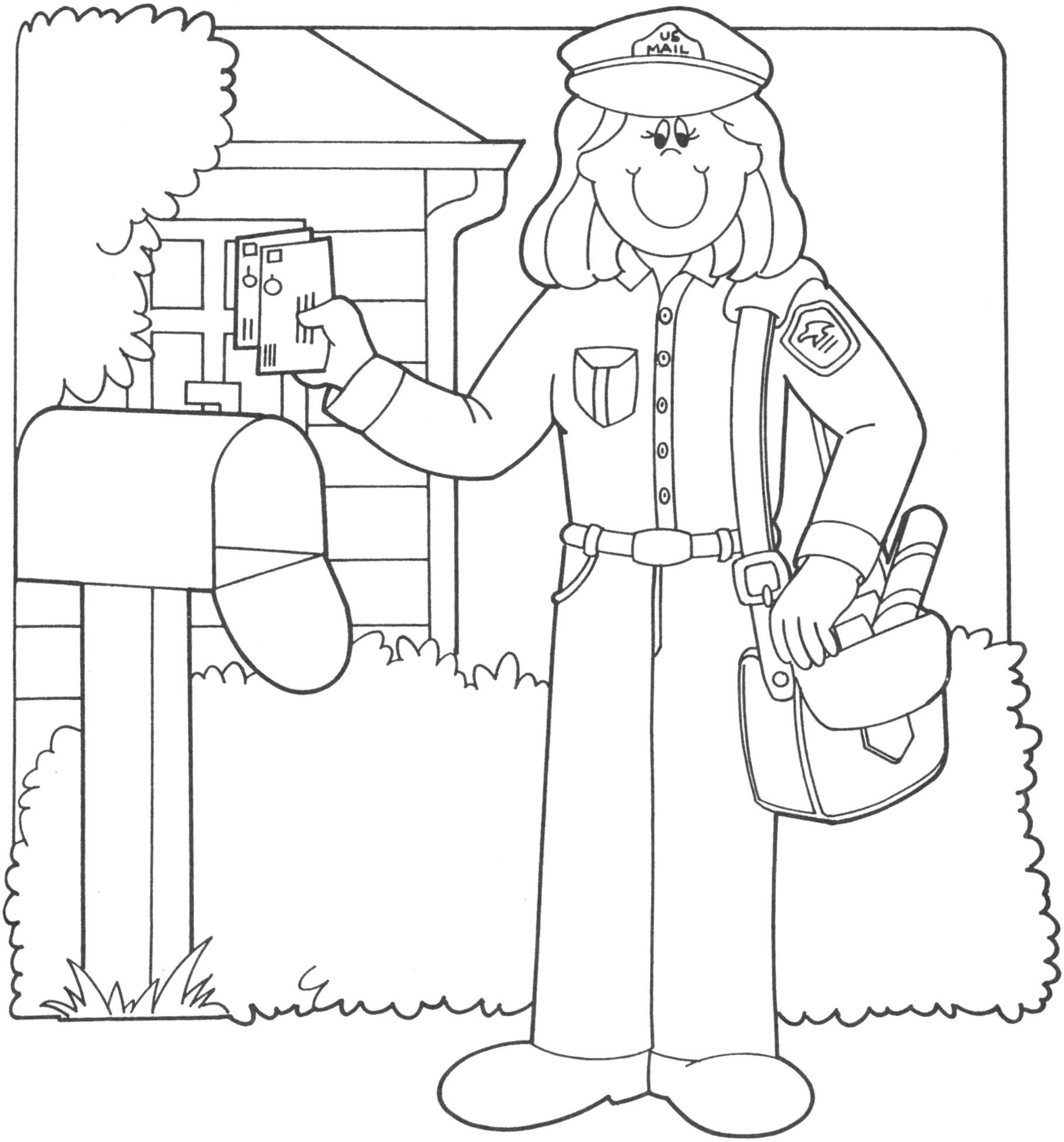

© Carson-Dellosa Publ. CD-6864

Draw lines to **match** the stamps.

The **dentist** helps us keep our teeth
So strong and pearly white.
When she says to brush and watch our sweets,
We know that she is right.

Color the picture.

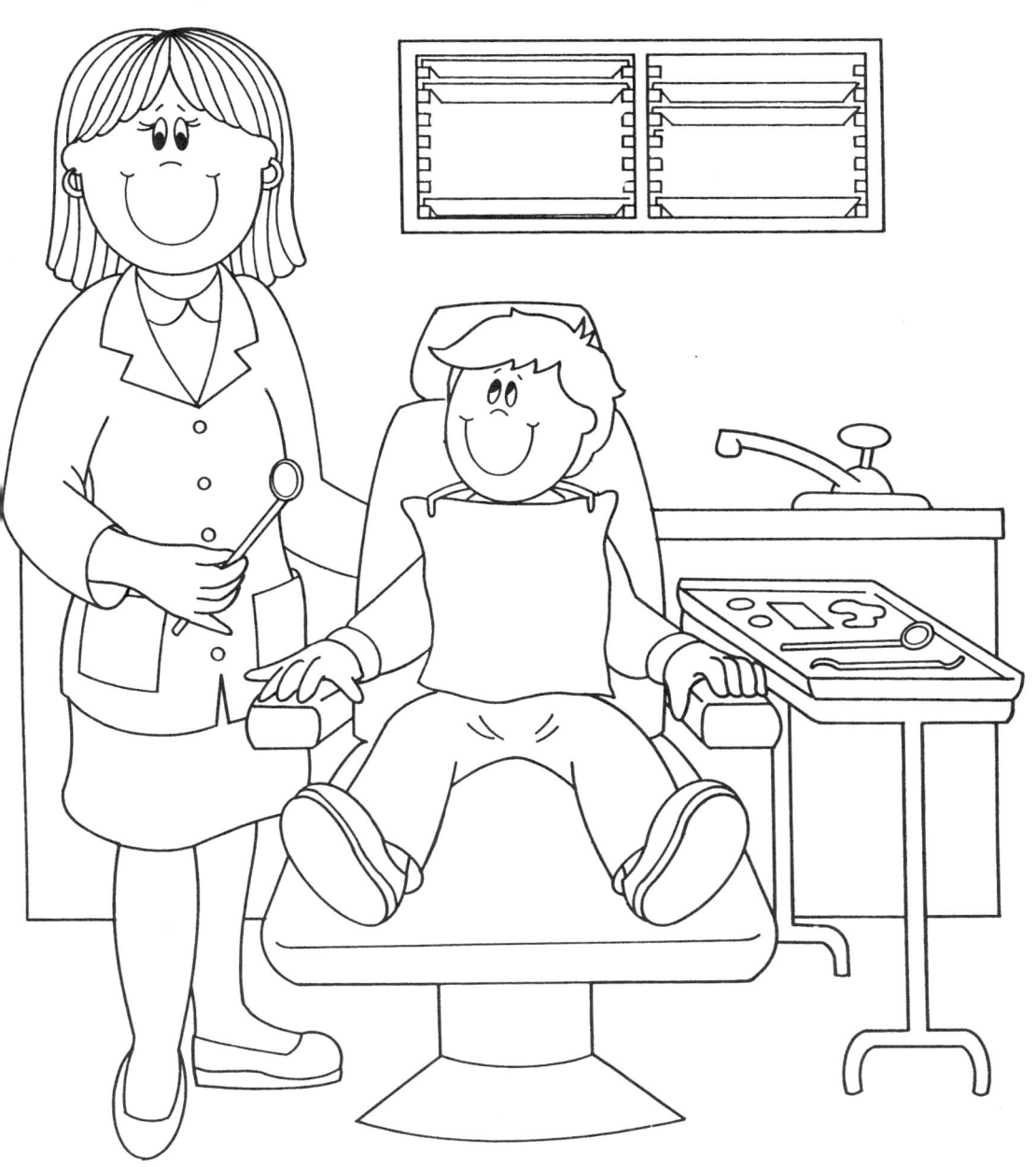

Circle the objects that are the same in each group.

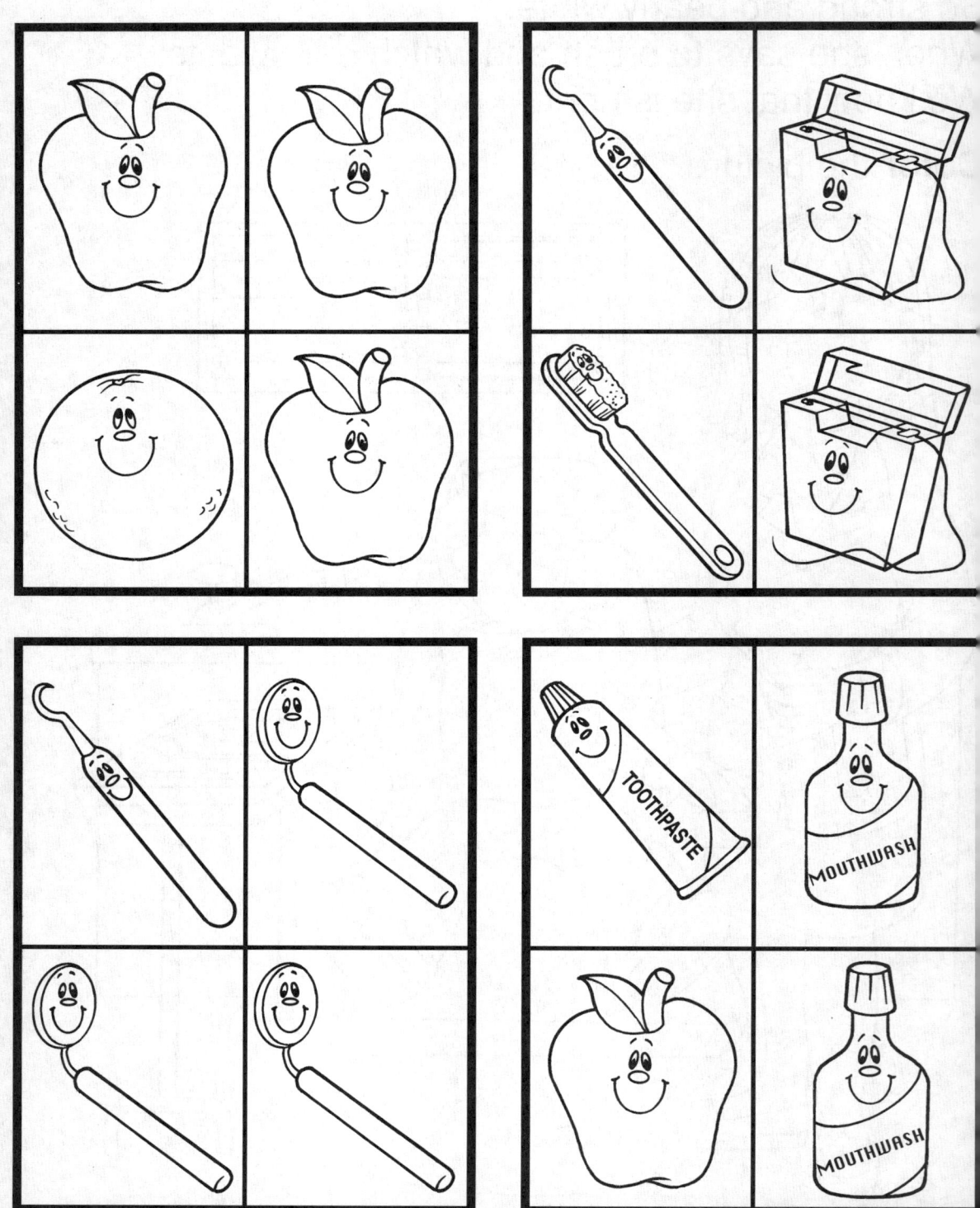

A **police officer** is someone
On whom we can depend
To keep our community safe and sound.
We know he is our friend.

Color the picture.

Count the number of objects in each box. **Print** the numeral on the line.

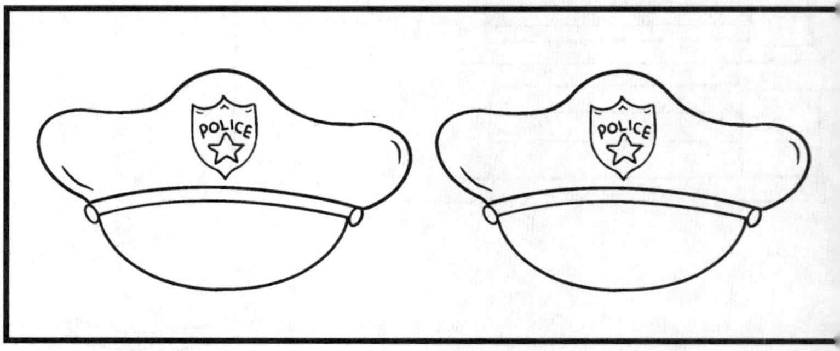

_____

_____

_____

_____

A **fire fighter's** job, we know,
Takes courage, strength, and speed.
He puts out fires and protects us
In our greatest times of need.

Color the picture.

Print the lowercase letter next to the uppercase letter.

Members of **Emergency Medical Services**

Have important jobs, we know.
One drives us safely to the hospital;
One cares for us as we go.

Color the picture.

Circle all the uppercase letters.

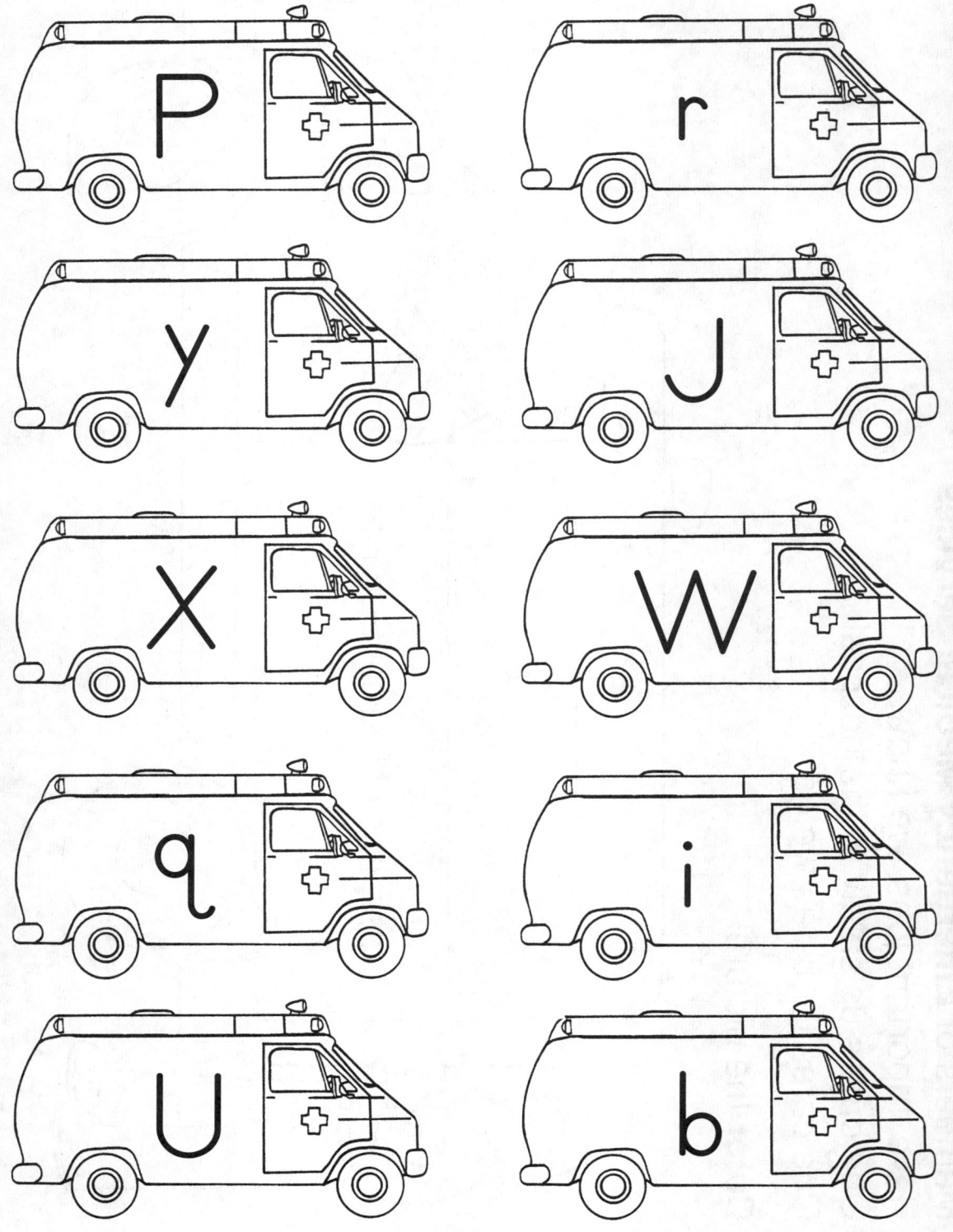

When we walk to school in our community,
It could be dangerous and quite hard,
But there's someone who makes it easy and safe,
And that is our **crossing guard**.

Color the picture.

Draw lines to **match** the signs.

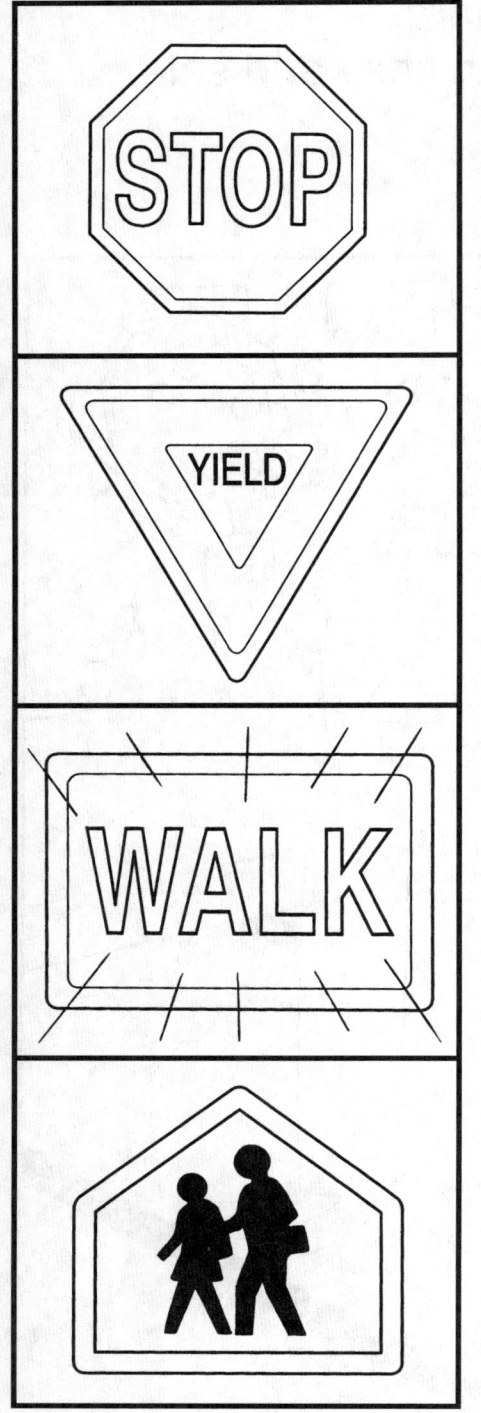

When we are ill or need a check-up,
Our **doctor** is the one that we see.
And she can make us feel better;
We're as thankful as we can be!

Color the picture.

Circle the objects that look like the first one in each row.

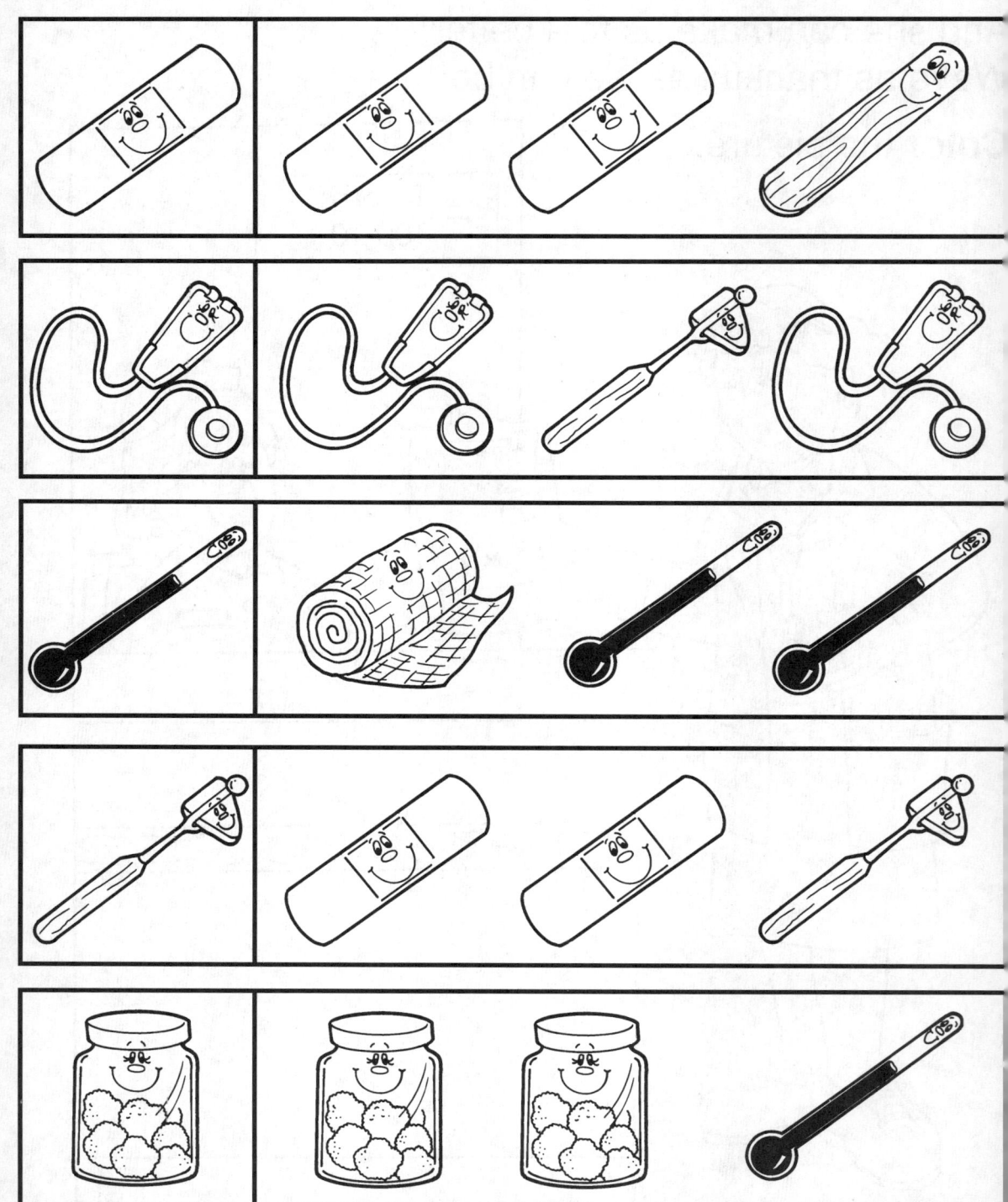

A **nurse's** job is aiding the doctor
In taking good care of the sick.
A good nurse is very important, you see,
Her special care does the trick!

Color the picture.

Draw lines to **match** the uppercase and lowercase letters.

H

R

A

Q

r

a

q

h

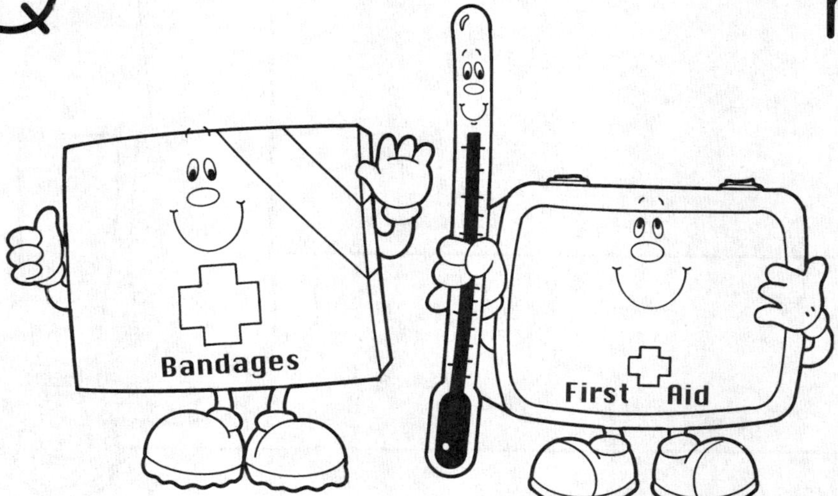

A **reporter** gets a story,
A scoop, a line, or the news,
For radio, T.V., or newspaper.
Listen, watch, or read— you choose.

Color the picture.

Print the uppercase letter next to each lowercase letter.

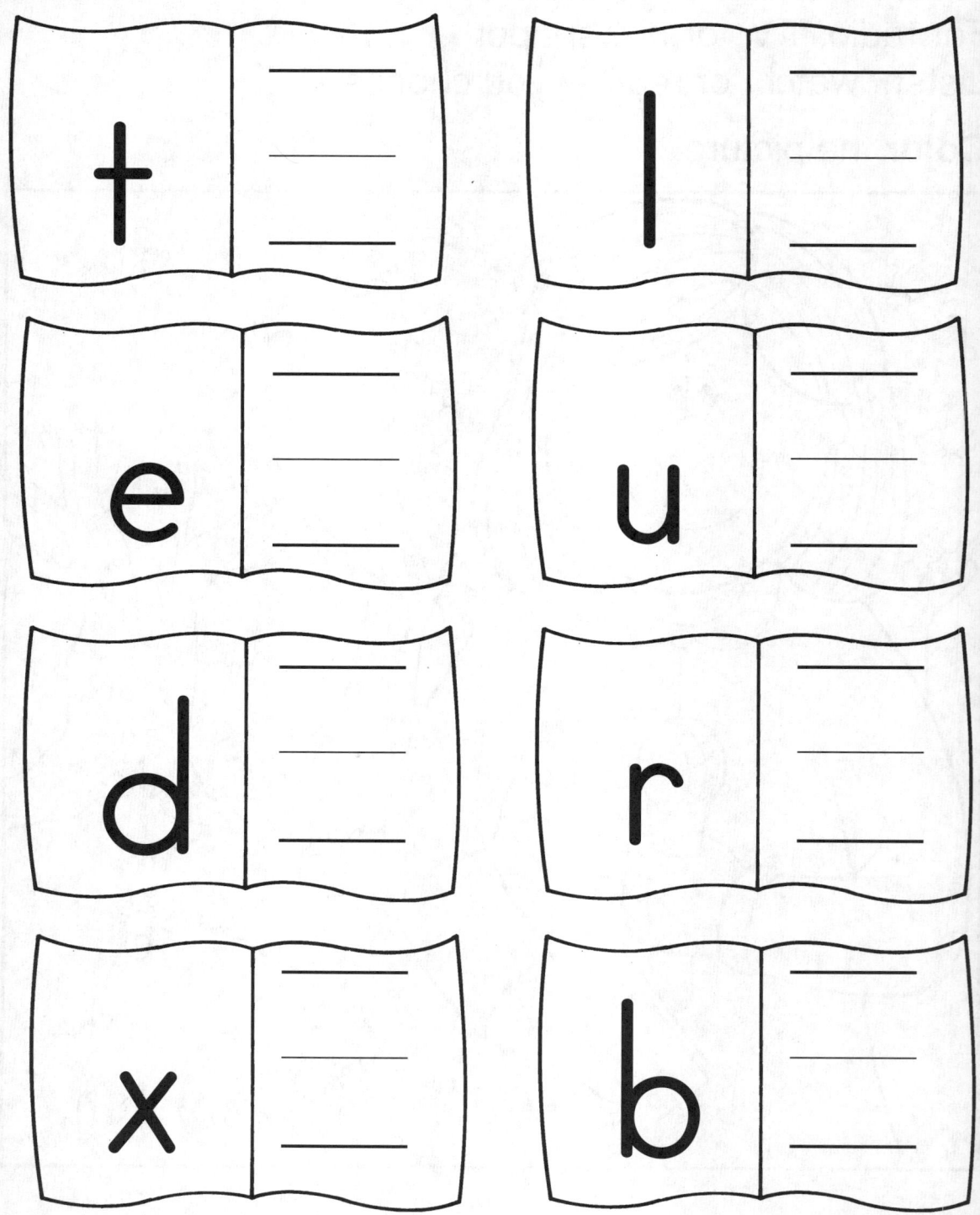

The **baker** is a community helper
We wouldn't want to be without;
Because it's his breads and pies and cakes
That we're always dreaming about.

Color the picture.

Circle the correct number of objects in each row.

5	(8 muffins)
2	(5 gingerbread men)
4	(6 donuts)
1	(3 loaves)
3	(4 pies)

The head of our community
Is the person who's called the **mayor**.
We count on this person that we voted in
To be honest, upstanding, and fair.

Color the picture.

Trace the letters. **Print** them on the lines below.

Thank goodness, the **dry cleaner** is near us
To clean our best sweaters and shirts.
Our clothes come back crisp, clean, and ironed
And rid of the worst kind of dirt.

Color the picture.

Color the sweaters that have uppercase letters **blue**.
Color the sweaters that have lowercase letters **red**.

If you have a tough legal problem—
A simple one will even do—
A **lawyer** is the community helper
Who'll give his assistance to you.

Color the picture.

Draw lines to match the letters.

B   P

G   B

H   G

P   H

The **farmer** gives us vegetables
And milk and grain and meat
And eggs and butter and fruit
And most of the things we eat!

Color the picture.

Circle the correct number of objects in each row.

| 5 |
| 3 |
| 2 |
| 1 |
| 4 |

A **truck driver** brings us many things
From places far and near.
She brings her goods to our neighborhood stores.
She's important to us and that's clear.

Color the picture.

Put an "X" over the truck that looks different in each group.

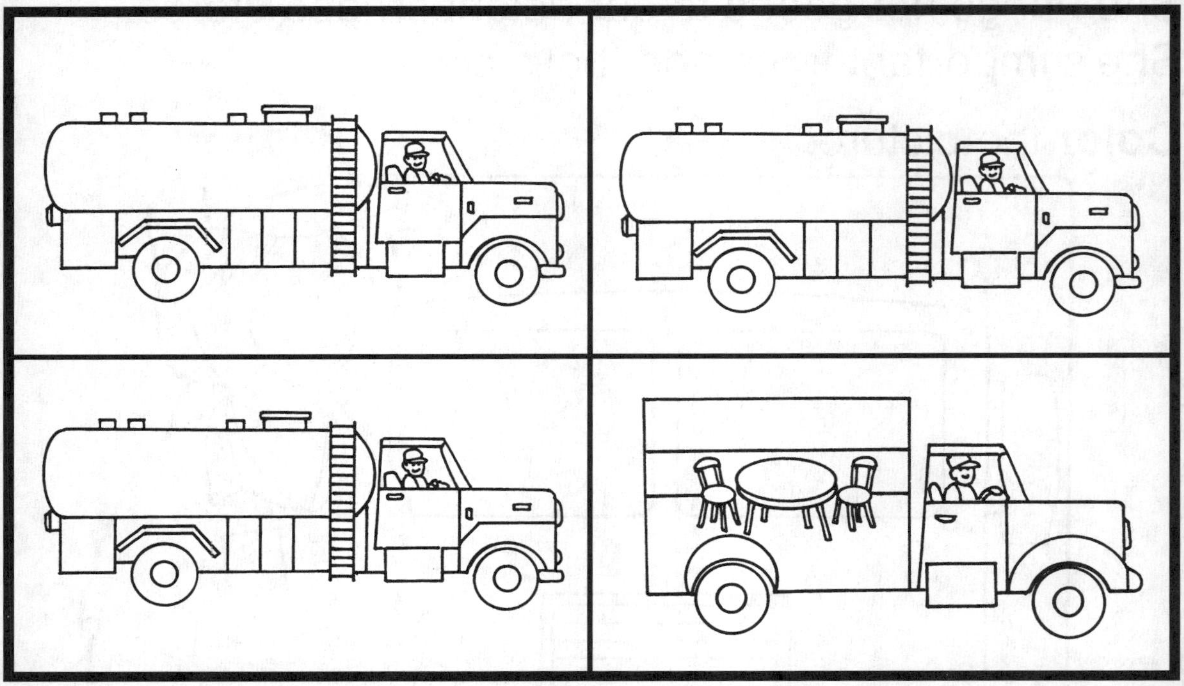

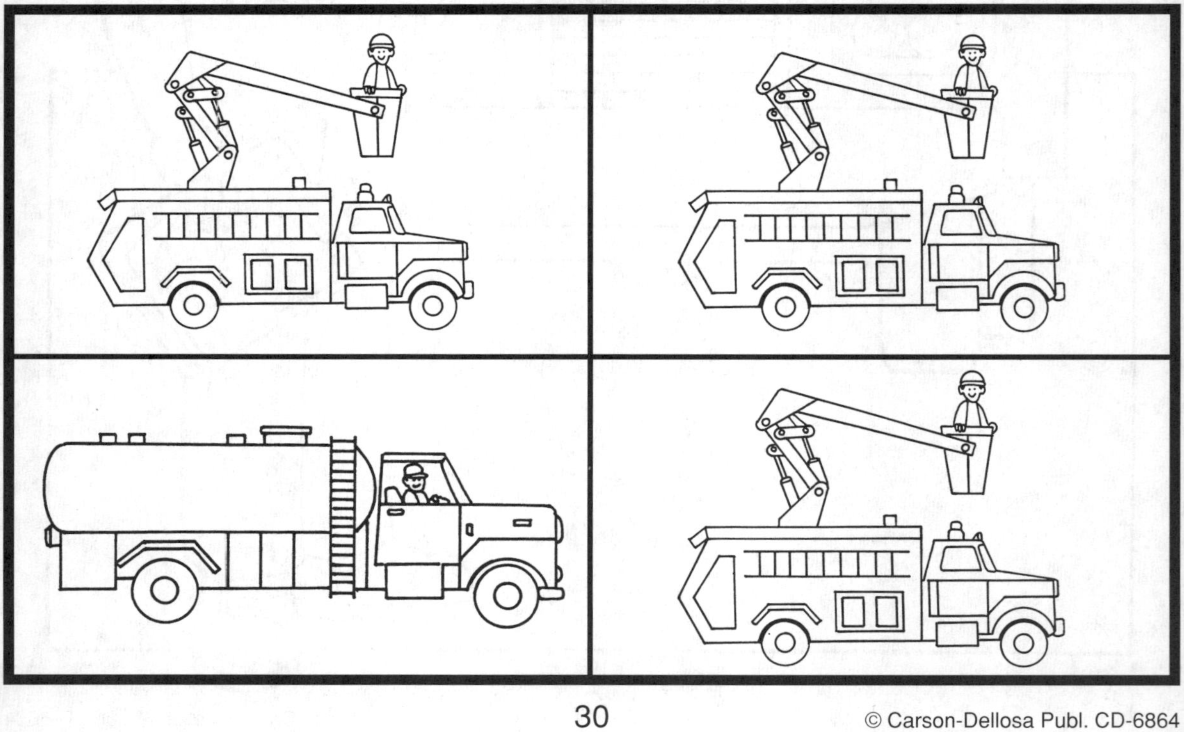

When you go to your favorite library
In search of a really special book,
The **librarian** is the one who can help you
By showing you just where to look.

Color the picture.

Look at the letters. **Print** the missing letter in each row.

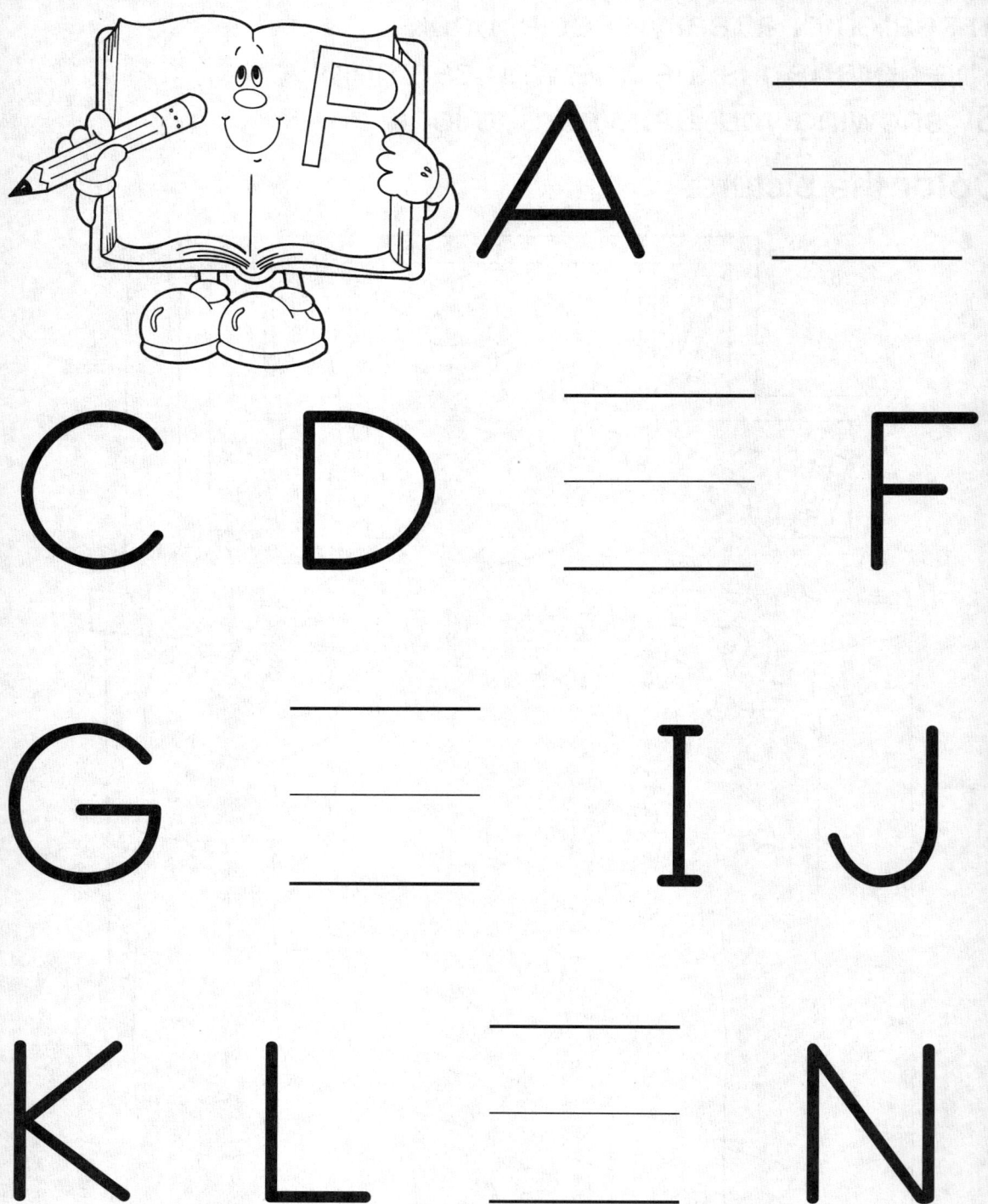

A _____

C D _____ F

G _____ I J

K L _____ N

Look at the letters. **Print** the missing letter in each row.

O P ___ R

S ___ U V

W ___

___ Z

Whether you go to a church or a temple,
A synagogue or a hall,
Your **church leader** is right there to help you,
And to help each of us, one and all.

Color the picture.

Use the color key below to **color** the picture.

Color Key:
1 – red   2 – green   3 – yellow   4 – blue

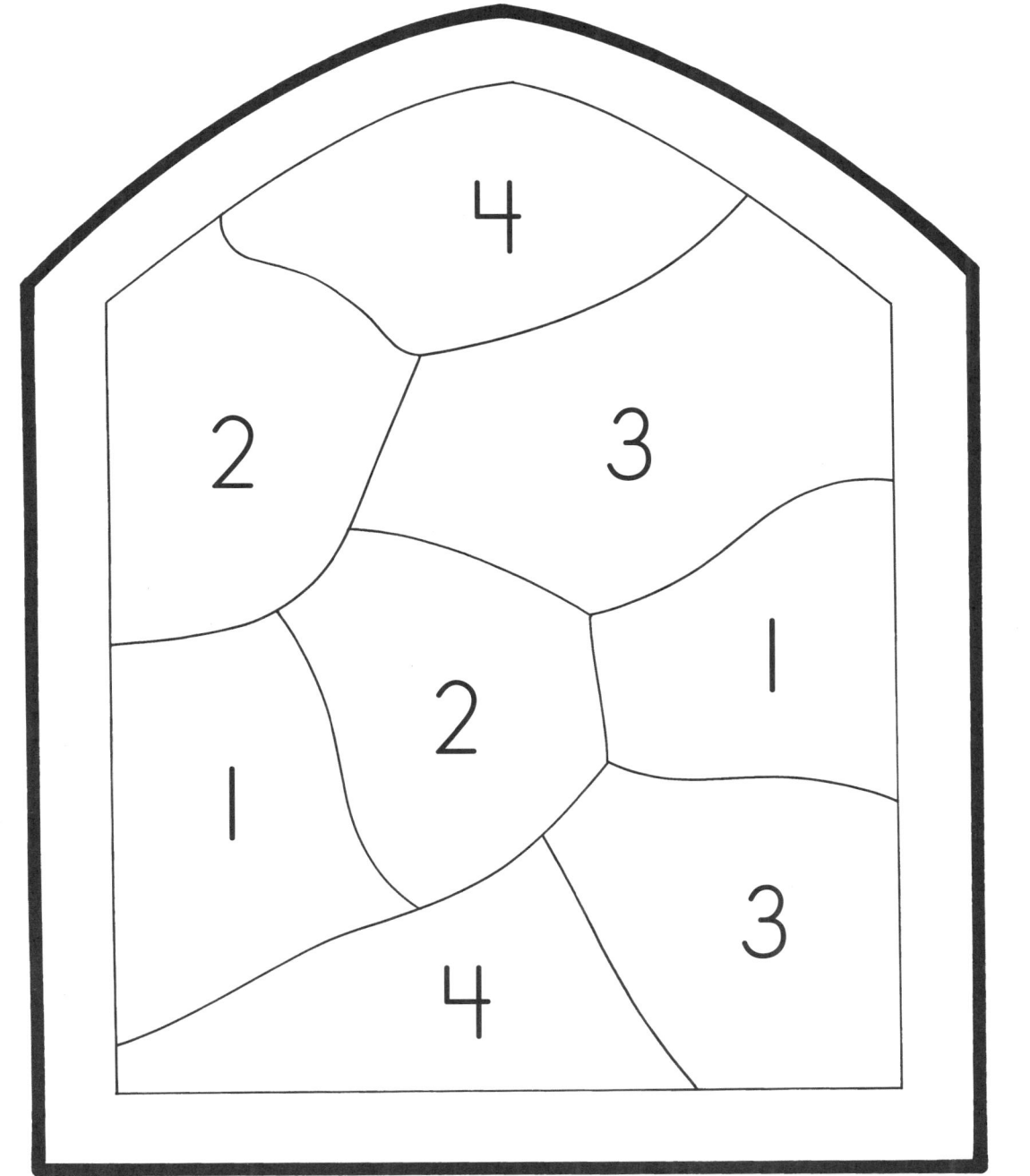

A **pharmacist** fills our prescriptions
And helps us when we need advice
About medicine that we might be taking.
She is always very busy, but nice.

Color the picture.

Look at the objects in each box. **Circle** the objects that look alike.

The **bank teller** is a good friend.
He works at the bank every day.
Whether we're spending or saving our money,
He is there to help show us the way.

Color the picture.

Look at each group. Draw lines to **connect** the groups that have the same number.

The **grocer** is the person we count on
For food and small things for our home.
He is always so helpful and we thank him
For each little kindness he has shown.

Color the picture.

Circle the correct number of objects in each row.

The **hairstylist** is someone who gives us
A haircut, a set, or a shampoo.
For ladies, men, or children,
She helps us to look fresh and new.

Color the picture.

Look at the pictures. **Put an "X"** over the picture or pictures that are different in each group.

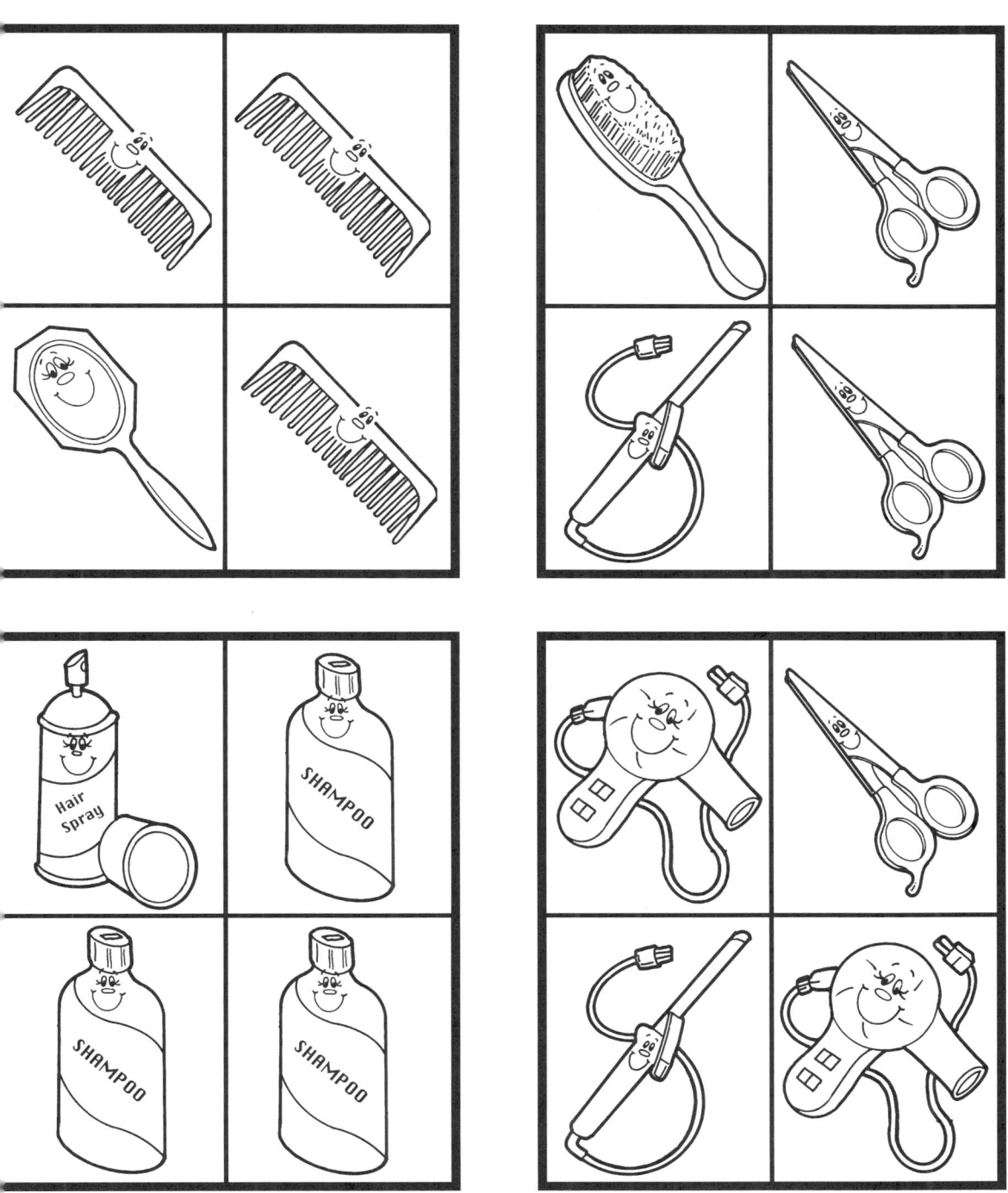

When our lovable pet is feeling ill,
The **veterinarian** is the one that we call.
For puppies, cats, birds, and bunnies,
The vet is the one who cares for them all.

Color the picture.

Match the numeral to the correct set.

10

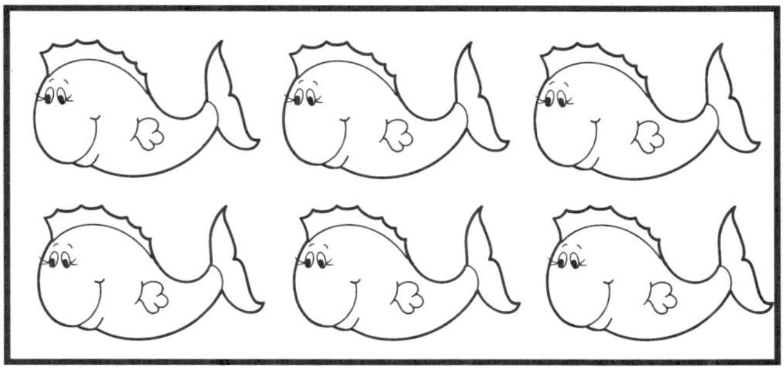

4

6

3

45

The Animal Control Officer

Rescues dogs and cats every day.
He takes them to animal shelters,
where they're loved and fed while they stay.

Color the picture.

Draw lines to **match** the pictures that look the same.

The **service station attendant**
Is the person who helps with our car.
He might change the oil or pump gas for us.
He helps us feel safe to drive far.

Color the picture.

Trace each numeral. Write the numeral on the line.

The **sanitation workers** are helpful, we know.
They pick up our refuse and trash.
They drive trucks all over our neighborhood
And clean up the mess in a flash.

Color the picture.

Match the numerals to the correct sets.

1

3

5

4

9

A **school bus driver** has a very big job,
Transporting so many to school.
We can help make her job so much simpler
By remembering to obey every rule!

Color the picture.

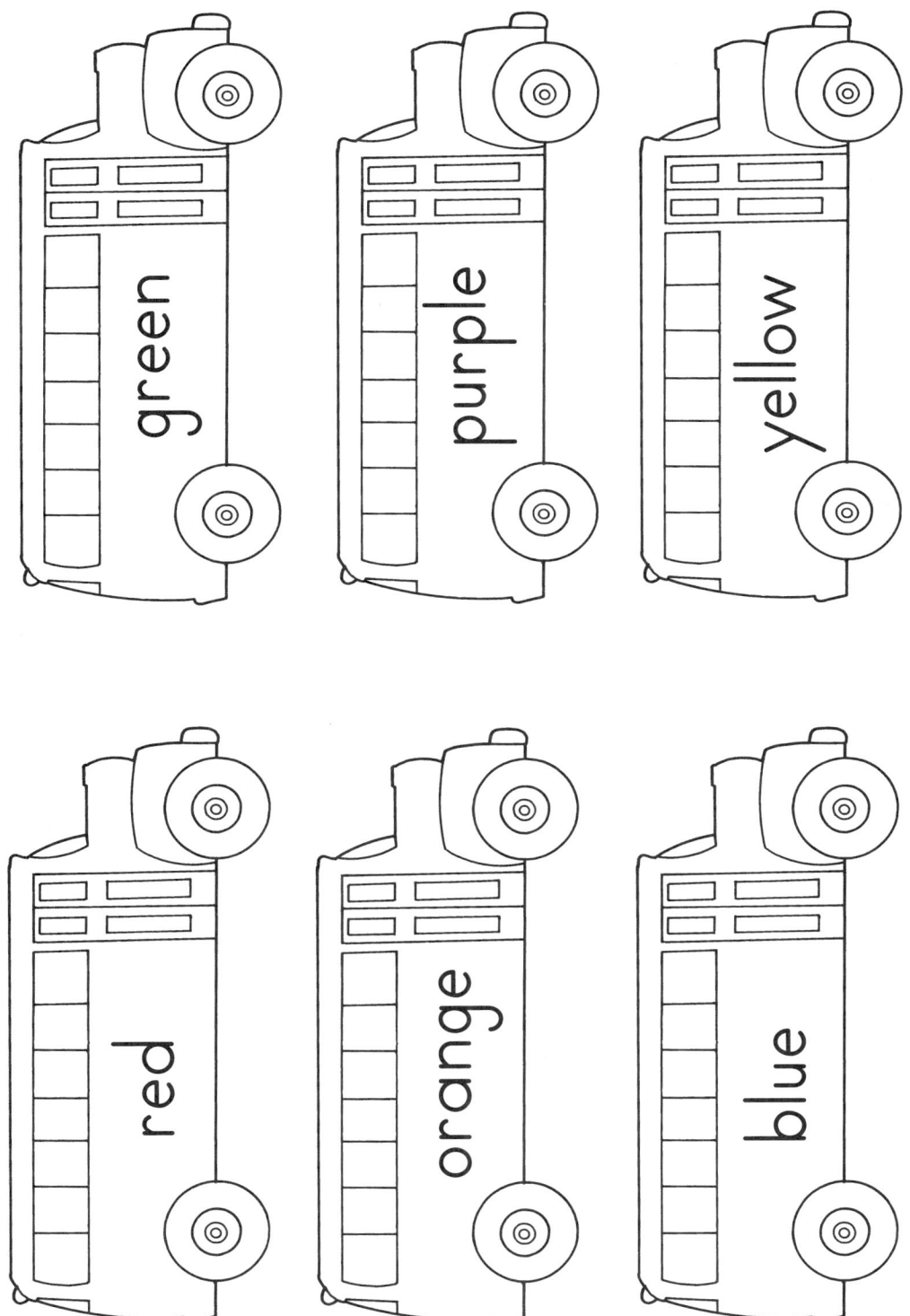

By sawing and nailing and drilling,
A **construction worker** can make quite a lot–
A home or a barn or an office.
We're glad for the talent he's got!

Color the picture.

CAUTION
CONSTRUCTION
SITE

Use the key below to color the picture.

A **zookeeper** cares for the animals
With food and tender care.
The animals all feel safe and sound
To know he is always there.

Color the picture.

Look at the letter in each box. **Circle** the picture or pictures that begin with the letter.

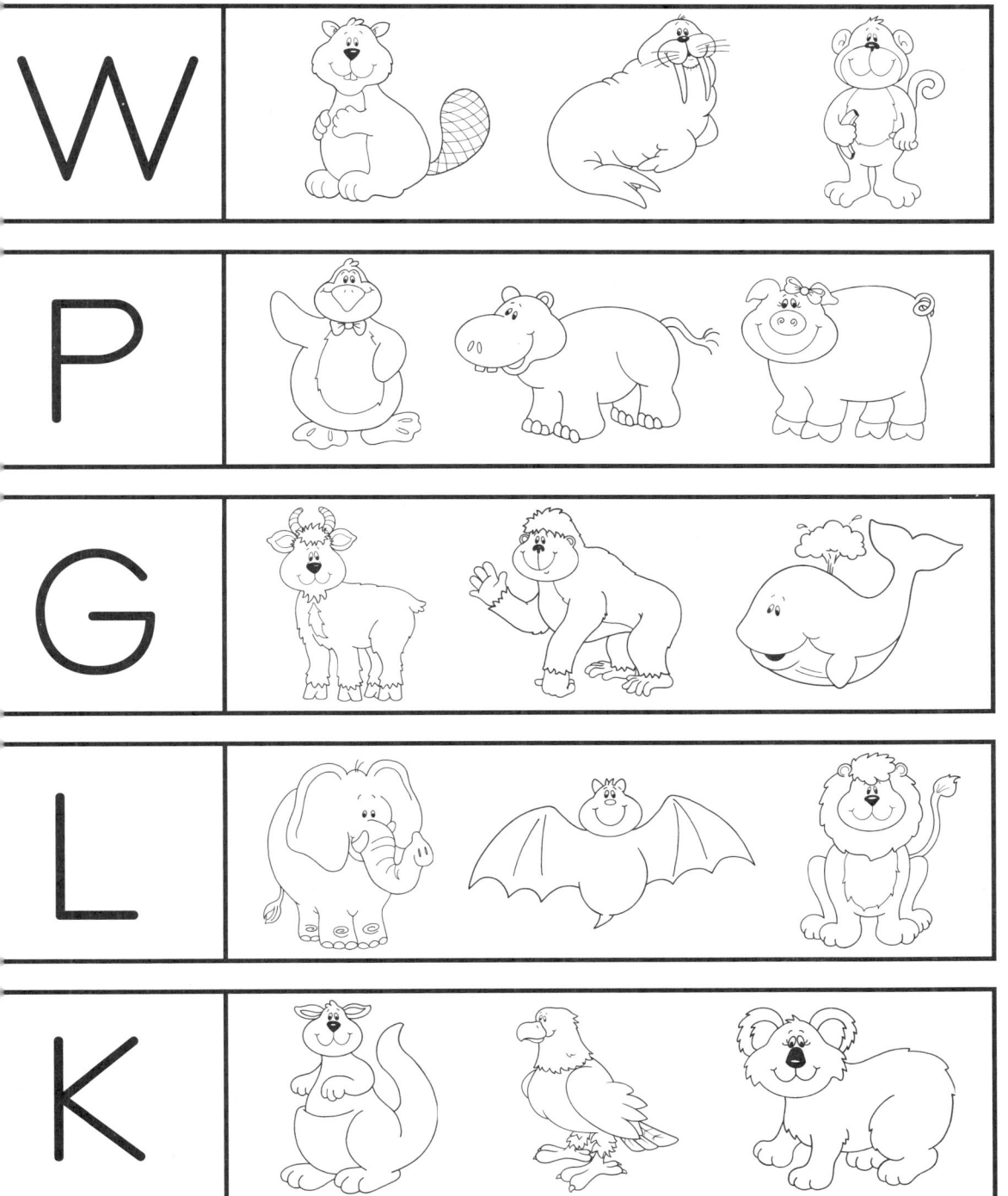

Our **newspaper carrier** is someone
Whose job can demand quite a lot.
She delivers our paper when the weather is nice,
And she does the same job when it's not!

Color the picture.

Count the newspapers in each group. **Print** the numeral on the line.

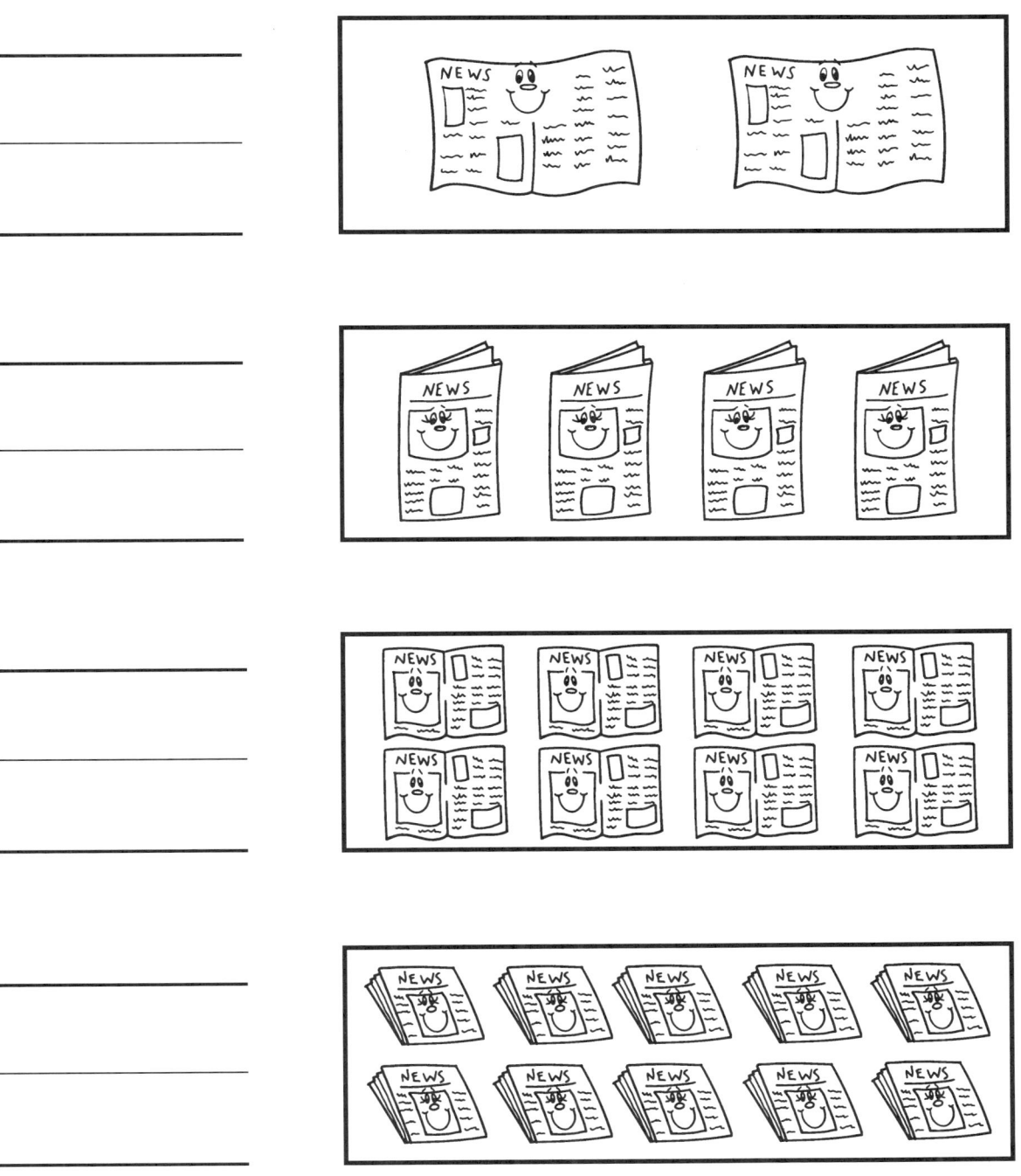

A **teacher** is an important helper.
Who teaches us how to say,
"Thank you," to our community helpers
For being there for us each day.

Color the picture.

Trace each letter. **Print** your own letter beside it.

Trace each letter. **Print** your own letter beside it.

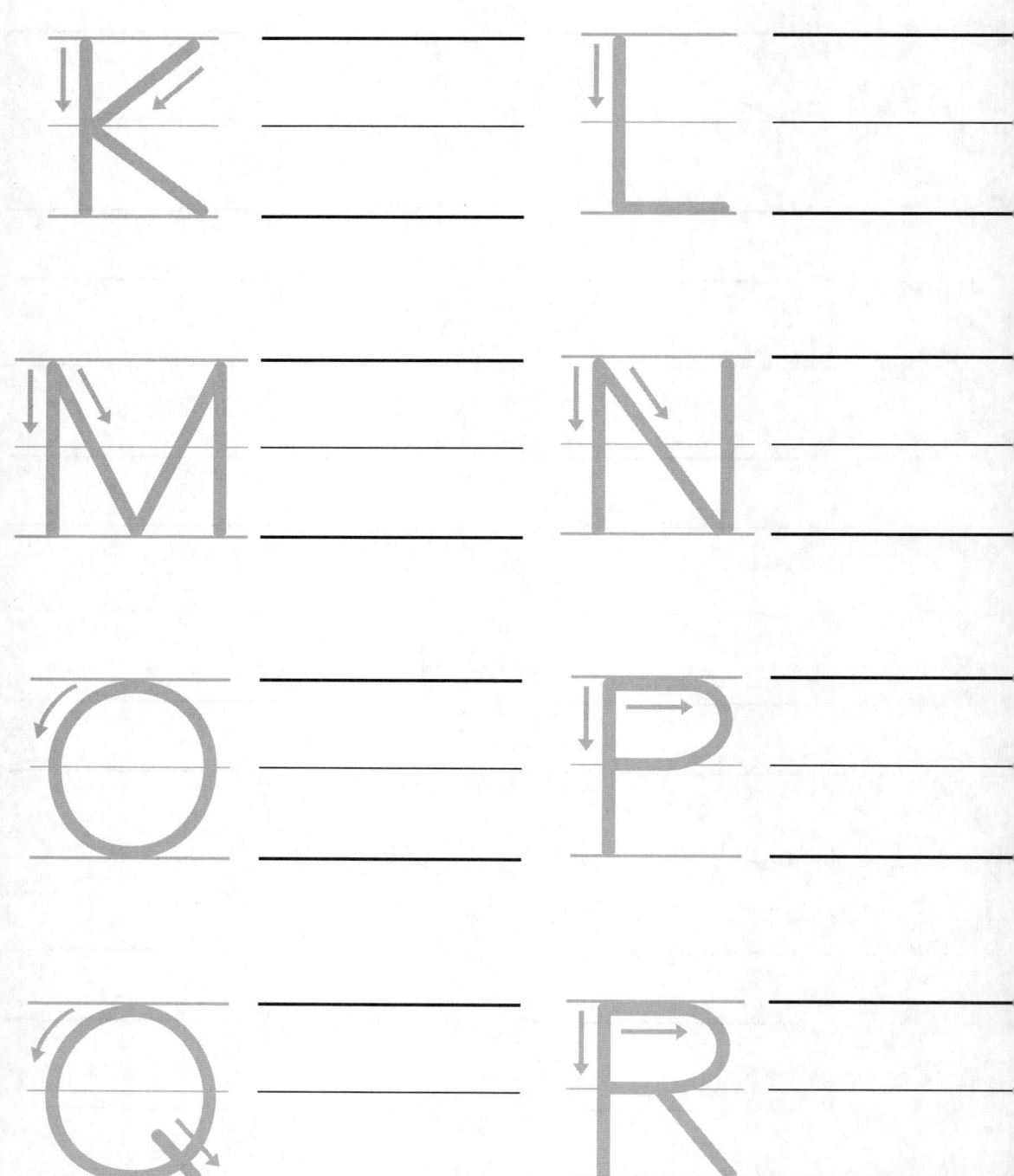

Trace each letter. **Print** your own letter beside it.

S _____ T _____

U _____ V _____

W _____ X _____

Y _____ Z _____

The **people who work in our community**
Help us in many ways.
We count on them to do certain jobs for us
Each and every day!

Color the picture.